Sound Trackers

Heavy Metal

SOUND TRACKERS – HEAVY METAL
was produced by

David West Children's Books
7 Princeton Court - 55 Felsham Road
London SW15 1AZ

Picture research: Brooks Krikler Research

Published in the United States in 1999 by Peter Bedrick Books
A division of NTC/Contemporary Publishing Group, Inc.
4255 West Touhy Avenue
Lincolnwood (Chicago), Illinois 60646-1975 U.S.A.

Library of Congress Cataloging-in-Publication Data

Brunning, Bob.
Heavy metal / Bob Brunning.
     p. cm. -- (Sound trackers)
   Summary: Examines notable recording artists of the heavy metal
movement, including AC/DC, Aerosmith, Black Sabbath, Alice Cooper,
Iron Maiden, Kiss, and Van Halen.
   ISBN 0-87226-580-3 (hc)
   1. Heavy metal (Music)--History and criticism Juvenile literature.
[1. Heavy metal (Music)--History and criticism. 2. Rock groups.
3.Musicians.]   I. Title. II. Series.
ML3534.8785 1999
781.66--dc21   99-27832
                                                                      CIP

Printed and Bound in Italy

International Standard Book Number: 0-87226-580-3

99 00 01 02 03 10 9 8 7 6 5 4 3 2 1

Heavy Metal

Bob Brunning

PETER BEDRICK BOOKS
NEW YORK

CONTENTS

On these discs is a selection of the artists' recordings. Many of these albums are now available on CD. If they are not, many of the tracks from them can be found on compilation CDs.

These boxes give you extra information about the music, the artists and performers, and their times. Some contain anecdotes about the artists themselves or the people who helped – or occasionally exploited – them. Others provide historical facts and fascinating insights into the music, lifestyles, fans, fads and fashions of the day.

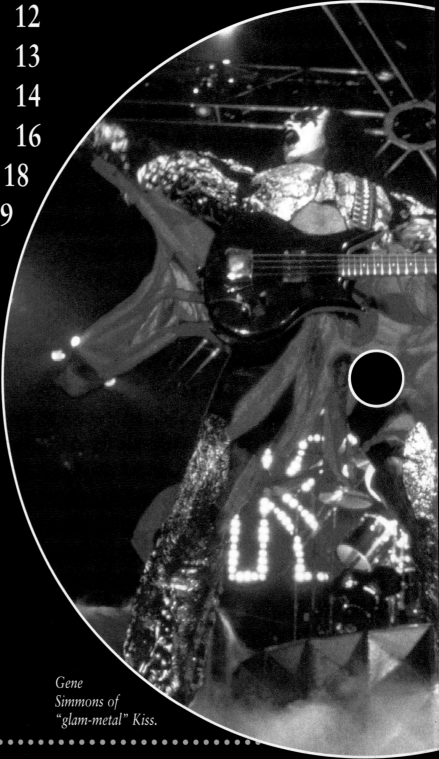

Gene Simmons of "glam-metal" Kiss.

INTRODUCTION

Some say that heavy metal is the easiest style of modern music to identify. But those closer to HM—or "metal"—say that it's the most difficult. So what, in general, are they talking about?

Phil Lynott of "folk metal" Thin Lizzy.

First, the name. *Heavy metal* was a phrase in a 1959 novel (see page 7). "Heavy" means the sounds are loud and deep. "Metal" is the metallic crashing of guitar strings. HM is usually guitar-led, often with fast, highly technical playing. Songs may be ponderously slow or thrashingly fast, with forceful, dramatic vocals, yells and roars.

Next, equipment. Guitars and drums are often customized (see page 17) . The back line (on-stage amplifiers and speakers for the band itself) is towering. The public address (sound system for the audience) is mountainous. Power = volume = energy.

Third, image. Often long hair, leather waistcoats and scruffy jeans, with plenty of macho posing, guitar waving and clenched fists. Some HM bands prefer extravagant theatrics, colorful make-up and glamorous costumes – or sinister darkness.

HM grew out of progressive and heavy rock from the late 1960s, with bands such as Cream, Led Zeppelin and Deep Purple. From 1976, Punk brought a competing type of loud, brash music. In the 1980s, some saw HM as "dinosaur rock." But its bands and fans have fought back, and heavy metal is once again popular, proud and loud.

AC/DC

Most young people cannot wait to get out of school uniforms. Angus Young, guitar-thrashing frontman from one of the first true heavy metal bands, did the reverse. He wore his uniform on stage, even short trousers and a cap! But then, AC/DC always stood by their own decisions. Their classic HM sound has endured for over 20 years.

THE WIZARDS FROM OZ

Often hailed as an Australian band, three key members of AC/DC were actually born in Scotland. Brothers Angus and Malcolm Young founded the band in Sydney, in 1973. Members came and went until 1976, when singer Bon (Ronald) Scott stabilized the line-up. Another Young brother, George – who had had success with the Easybeats' pop classic "Friday On My Mind" – helped set up a recording contract with the Australian company Albert. But the first three albums and seven singles, released only in Australia, hardly set the rock scene on fire.

Angus Young plays lead guitar.

ROCK THE WORLD

Nevertheless, the band had confidence in its loud, high-energy stage act. To achieve true stardom, they decided to spread out from Australia. In 1977, with Mark Evans (bass) and Phil Rudd (drums), they recorded "Let There Be Rock."

Then, with Cliff Williams (of Romford, Essex) replacing Evans, they toured Europe and North America. Success! The album entered the Top 20 in December. 1978's "Powerage" did less well, but the next year's "Highway To Hell" blasted into the Top 10. However, disaster struck on February 20, 1980 when Scott choked to death after heavy drinking. After some soul searching, the rest of AC/DC decided to carry on and signed up Brian Johnson, whose vocals were uncannily like Scott's.

Johnson's trademark is a flat cloth cap.

"Let There Be Rock"
October '77
"Highway To Hell"
August '79
"Back In Black" July '80
"For Those About To Rock (We Salute You)"
November '81

"Flick Of The Switch" August '83
"The Razor's Edge" October '90
"Box Set" August '91
"Live" October '92
"Ballbreaker"
September '95

A LIKING FOR LEATHER
The phrase *heavy metal* was derived from a quote by William Burroughs, about "heavy metal thunder," in his 1959 novel *The Naked Lunch*. Soon HM became associated with other dark, strong, tough, powerful, macho-style "heavy" subjects such as motorcycles, leather clothes, chrome, chains and semi-military uniforms. The 1970s trend towards "glam" brought sparkle, glitter, make-up and a slightly more camp or effeminate image. This was adopted by some HM performers. But the basic heavy leather look is still popular, with HM artists and followers alike.

Judas Priest, popular from the late '70s to about 1990, model the HM leather look.

BACK TO BLACK HITS
1980 also saw AC/DC's first No. 1 album, "Back In Black." In '81 "For Those Who Are About To Rock (We Salute You)" sold massively, and a scorching performance at HM's premier festival, Castle Donington, established AC/DC as one of the world's top heavy metal bands. There have been personnel changes since, but Top 10 albums continue to flow, including "Live" which topped video sales too. The Youngs and Johnson continue to rock, and Angus still has not grown out of his school uniform …

AEROSMITH

Any type of music has its purer and simpler styles, and its more complicated, involved ones. Aerosmith combine both. They are one of the more clever tricksy HM bands, with lengthy songs arranged into various linked sections, and rapid changes of pace and rhythm that swap keys and riffs at speed. Some people would argue that they are not truly "metal." They are heavy rock, and too clever for their own boots ...

EARLY PROBLEMS

Joey Kramer, Aerosmith's drummer from the beginning, came up with the band name by mixing letters in the style of the board word game Scrabble. Joey, with vocalist Steven Tyler and guitarist Joe Perry, considered two possibilities – Songsmith and Aerospace. They mixed the two and luckily chose the better combination. The band's first incarnation was as a fairly standard heavy rock outfit in the late 1970s. But drink and drugs took their toll. Aerosmith's career began to falter during the 1980s. The songwriting duo of Tyler and Perry lost their knack of creating tunes that were tough yet smart.

Substance abuse earned songwriters Tyler (left) and Perry (right) the nickname of "Toxic Twins."

WAKING UP

Despite their problems, Aerosmith have boasted an exceptionally stable line-up over many years. Natural frontman Tyler on vocals, keyboards and other instruments, plus the thoughtful Perry and super-rapid drummer Kramer, are accompanied by Brad Whitford on rhythm guitar and Tom Hamilton on bass. In 1987 "Permanent Vacation" showed a newer, sharper version of the band. The same year rappers Run DMC had a huge hit single with "Walk This Way." The song had been written by Tyler and Perry, and had featured on an earlier Aerosmith recording.

"Permanent Vacation"
August '87
"Pump"
September '89
"Get A Grip"
April '93

"Big Ones"
November '94
"Nine Lives"
March '97

METAL WOMEN

The place of females in heavy metal music has always been confusing. Pretty girls have been added to mainly-male HM bands for decoration, presumably to lure more male HM fans. Several female vocalists have explored the heavy sound, notably Joan Jett and the Blackhearts in the USA, who had a single hit in 1982 with "I Love Rock 'n' Roll," and UK band Girlschool. Alannah Myles' 1989 album of the same name boasted her smouldering, bluesy hit "Black Velvet," but most of the rest was raucous and metal-like. However, in the area of sexual equality, it could be argued that HM still has a long way to go.

Girlschool charted in 1981 with "Hit 'n' Run."

BETTER, BETTER

Aerosmith developed their theme of heavy-but-clever songs with a vengeance, assisted by a colorful stage show topped by Tyler's tall hat. Their '89 album "Pump" included the 5-minutes-21-seconds "Love In An Elevator," an established classic in mini-opera format. It still appears regularly on lists of all-time great rock songs.

The band's fortunes soared with a guest appearance at "Waynestock" in the cult movie "Wayne's World 2." In 1994 a release of earlier tracks reminded listeners that Aerosmith had always harbored talent and showmanship. As some areas of heavy metal become musically more complex, but without losing the essential strong riffs and pounding beats, Aerosmith are elder statesmen who continue to lead from the front.

BLACK SABBATH

Heavy metal is sometimes linked with black magic, curses, spells and the Devil. Partly responsible are one of the "founding father" bands of HM, still regarded as among the loudest and heaviest. Black Sabbath can hardly argue against the case. Their name was inspired by bassist Terry "Geezer" Butler's interest in Dennis Wheatley's 1960s novel "The Devil Rides Out."

"Black Sabbath" February '70
"Paranoid" September '70
"Master Of Reality" August '71
"Sabbath Bloody Sabbath" November '73
"Sabotage" September '75

"Technical Ecstasy" October '76
"Heaven And Hell" April '80
"Live At Last" June '80
"Born Again" September '83
"Dehumaniser" June '92

CHANGE OF TUNE

Ozzy Osbourne is still successfully solo in 1998.

In 1967, singer John Michael "Ozzy" Osbourne joined up with guitarist Tony Iommi, Butler on bass and drummer Bill Ward. Known by various hippie-inspired names such as Mythology and Whole Earth, they dabbled in musical styles such as jazz and blues. But as their own ponderous, riff-laden, pile-driving sound took shape, they adopted the name Black Sabbath, and in 1970 moved to the progressive Vertigo label. Their powerful dark image, immensely loud stage show and relentless touring paid off, and the first album "Black Sabbath" made the Top 10 in March. The single "Paranoid" from the second chart-topping album of the same name has become an all-time HM classic.

COURTING CONTROVERSY

Wakeman brought the organ sound.

The Birmingham-based quartet's controversial approach to musical content, including substance abuse and mental illness, led to widespread criticism. The band were accused of encouraging drugs or even suicide. Nevertheless their first six albums (to 1975) made the Top 10, and in 1973 they were joined by ex-Yes keyboardist Rick Wakeman.

Gradually success waned, despite exhausting global tours. Musical differences surfaced and Ozzy Osborne left temporarily in late 1977, then for good in '78. American Ronnie James Dio sang on 1978's "Never Say Die." In spite of his impressive track record (see page 15), he was gone by 1982, replaced by Ian Gillan. Ward also left, and in came Vinnie Appice, brother of Carmine Appice, acclaimed drummer in Vanilla Fudge. 1983 saw the arrival of keyboard player Geoff Nichols, Glenn Hughes on vocals, bassist Dave Spitz and drummer Eric Singer.

REGROUPING

The musicianship was still first-class, but the magic and fan base were evaporating, with only Tony Iommi from the original group. Another drummer who passed through Sabbath's ranks was the hugely experienced Cozy Powell (see panel, right). In 1991 Iommi attempted to recreate the band's original line-up and persuaded Butler, but drummer Ward refused. With Ronnie James Dio back again, the re-vamped Sabbath entered the Top 30 with "Tyr" and "Dehumaniser." Despite their '90s fade-out, Black Sabbath richly deserve their place as one of HM's all-time greats.

POWELL POWER

Cozy Powell became Black Sabbath's drummer during the late 1980s. In April 1998 he sadly died in a car crash near his Bristol home. Cozy was a phenomenally fast, energetic drummer with a pivotal role in British heavy metal music. In addition to Black Sabbath, he played and recorded with Whitesnake, Rainbow, ELP (Emerson Lake and Powell), Jeff Beck, the Michael Shenker Group, Roger Daltrey and, perhaps surprisingly, '60s folk singer Donovan. He also had single hits – featuring massive drum sounds, of course – including "Dance With The Devil" in 1973. Powell could be argumentative, arrogant and opinionated, which often helps in the rock music business. Yet he could also be kind and considerate. He shared his vast experience and understanding with many younger drummers and percussionists.

Powerhouse drummer Cozy Powell.

ALICE COOPER

From the name "Alice Cooper," you might picture a quiet lady singing folksy ballads. Instead, you got a deafeningly heavy rock band, screams and wails, piercing guitar feedback, and a horrific stage show featuring zombies, axes, chainsaws and dripping blood. The lead singer even pretended to saw off his own arm or fry in his on-stage electric chair.

"Killer" January '72
"School's Out" July '72
"Billion Dollar Babies" March '73
"Welcome To My Nightmare" March '75

"Alice Cooper Goes To Hell" July '76
"Constrictor" October '86
"Trash" August '89
"The Last Temptation" June '94

FROM VINCENT TO ALICE

For "Alice" was a he – Vincent Damon Furnier. At first the band was called Alice Cooper. They began as a reasonably successful heavy group, but by about 1970 they needed a kick-start. In came glam-horror, with ghoulish make-up, sinister lyrics about murder and mutilation, and a fright-a-minute stage act with snakes and other sinister symbols. There were reports of on-stage Alice beheading live chickens (actually fakes) and ripping blood-spurting limbs off toy dolls. Members of the audience fainted, vomited or walked out.

THEATER, NOT MUSIC

But the shock tactics worked. After a low-20s hit in early 1972, the follow-up "School's Out" made Top 5 in the albums chart, and the single of the same name went to No. 1. In 1973 the fourth album of this period, "Billion Dollar Babies," was at No. 1 in the UK for almost half the year. In 1975, Furnier took the group's name for himself. Critics suggested his music needed shock-horror theatrics for success. In reply, Alice has continued his themes and songs, though lately more tongue-in-cheek. In the 1990s he has broken into the Top 5 with several albums, including 1991's "Hey Stoopid."

CREAM

Cream was born out of the "blues boom" in mid-1960s Britain. They took blues, made it into loud rock, added power chords, riffs and lengthy solos, and helped to forge the sound of heavy metal.

"Fresh Cream" December '66
"Disraeli Gears" November '67
"Wheels Of Fire" August '68

"Goodbye Cream" March '69
"Live Cream" June '70
"Strange Brew: Best Of Cream" February '83

THE POWER TRIO

Cream's bassist Jack Bruce and drummer Ginger Baker came from jazz backgrounds, while blues fan Eric Clapton became the UK's first "guitar hero" in John Mayall's Bluesbreakers. Clapton wanted to experiment and, impressed by their skills, invited Bruce and Baker to form a new style of band – the power trio. Cream was born in 1966.

TRIALS AND TENSIONS

The band's first album "Fresh Cream" peaked at No. 5 in the UK album charts. A furious touring schedule ensued, but problems soon developed. Bruce and Baker had a history of arguments and even fist-fights. Yet on stage, these tensions seemed to help their music. The trio constantly extended and improvised their basic songs in the style of jazz musicians, with screaming notes from Clapton, Bruce playing bass like a lead guitar, and Baker developing 20-minute drum solos.

But it was very short-lived. Cream released seven singles and only three proper studio albums plus various "live" versions. Thankfully their last concert at London's Albert Hall was captured on film. The inevitable split came on November 26, 1968 and left hordes of high-energy power-players heading towards true HM.

After Cream, Clapton (right) and Baker (center-right) formed another "supergroup," Blind Faith.

DEEP PURPLE

In April 1968, after intensive rehearsals in a Hertfordshire farmhouse, a new heavy band prepared to hit the road. But the members were cautious, and decided to debut away from the UK, in case they flopped. This is why Jon Lord, Ritchie Blackmore, Ian Paice, Rod Evans and Nick Simper played their first gig in a school hall in Tastrup, Denmark. Called Roundabout, the band soon changed its name. A heavy metal legend was born.

CLASSICAL AND ROCK

That first 11-date Danish tour was a modest success, and Deep Purple signed to Parlophone. Influenced by the American band Vanilla Fudge, their first two albums, "Shades Of Deep Purple" and "Book Of Taliesyn," featured extravagant re-workings of famous rock songs. Virtually ignored in the UK, they made the Top 10 in the USA. By 1969 guitarist Blackmore and keyboardist Lord were writing their own songs. Evans and Simper departed, replaced by vocalist Ian Gillan and bassist Roger Glover. After an unsteady rock-classical fusion "Concerto For Group And Orchestra" came the HM classic, "Deep Purple In Rock." In 1970, the single "Black Night" went to No. 2 in the UK.

"Shades Of Deep Purple" September '68
"Deep Purple In Rock" June '70
"Fireball" September '71
"Machine Head" April '72
"Made In Japan" December '72
"Burn" February '74

"Stormbringer" November '74
"Deep Purple Live" November '76
"Deepest Purple" (compilation) July '80
"Perfect Strangers" November '84
"The House Of Blue Light" January '87
"The Battle Rages On" July '93

Ritchie Blackmore used extensive effects such as feedback and tremolo.

The next two albums, "Fireball" and "Machine Head," both went one better. The latter included the enduring HM anthem with one of rock's most famous guitar riffs, "Smoke On The Water." However, egos clashed again. Gillan and Glover quit, replaced by singer David Coverdale – plucked from Lancashire obscurity – and bassist Glenn Hughes.

Purple line-up from left to right: Lord, Blackmore, Glover, Gillan and Paice.

FADED PURPLE

In 1974 "Burn" and "Stormbringer" made the Top 10, and Purple undertook massive world tours. But their direction and impetus were fading. In 1975 Blackmore left (see panel). In came jazz-influenced Tommy Bolin for the twelfth album, "Come Taste The Band." Tragically he died of drug abuse two years later. Gillan, Lord, Blackmore, Glover and Paice reformed Deep Purple in the 1980s, with some commercial success, but the original fire and energy were lacking. Ian Gillan was soon on his way once more. Despite their many changes, Deep Purple richly deserve their status as one of heavy metal's most exciting and innovative bands.

PURPLE SPIN-OFFS

Various members of Deep Purple have enjoyed post-Purple success. Pyrotechnic guitarist Ritchie Blackmore founded Rainbow, whose first album of that name made the Top 10 in 1975. His scorchingly fast style, featuring notes from strings bent almost beyond belief, has been imitated but never bettered. A bewildering number of musicians passed through Rainbow, and their 1986 compilation "Finyl Album" reflects Blackmore's immense contribution to the heavy metal scene. Ian Gillan formed his own band Gillan, and also sang with Black Sabbath. In 1978 David Coverdale founded yet another long-lasting HM outfit, Whitesnake.

Rainbow featured Ronnie James Dio on vocals.

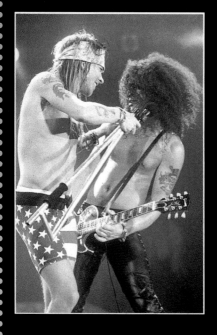

GUNS N' ROSES

William Bailey, born in 1962 in Lafayette, Indiana, USA, started his performing career at the tender age of five – singing in his local church choir. However, the church's influence faded as Bailey became immersed in the loud, fast, exciting rock music broadcast by the USA's innumerable radio stations. In 1984 he teamed up with like-minded guitarist Jeffrey Isbell in Los Angeles. The two decided to form a band. First on the list were stage names. William and Jeffrey just would not do …

GETTING THE NAMES RIGHT

… So Bailey became Axl Rose, and Isbell re-titled himself Izzy Stradlin. With Tacii Guns on guitar and Rob Gardner on drums, they needed a band name. First it was Hollywood Rose, then LA Guns, but neither seemed quite right. In any case, Guns and Gardner left. Drummer Steven Adler joined, along with guitarist Saul Hudson, a native of Stoke-on-Trent, England. More name changes followed. Hudson became Slash, and the band became Guns N' Roses. With Duff McKagan on bass, "Gee-En-Arr" hit the road with a vengeance.

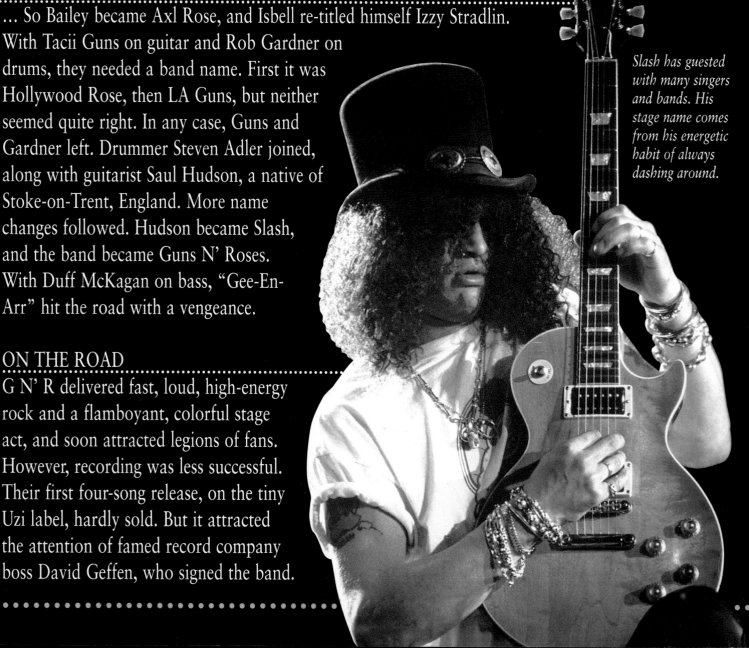

Slash has guested with many singers and bands. His stage name comes from his energetic habit of always dashing around.

ON THE ROAD

G N' R delivered fast, loud, high-energy rock and a flamboyant, colorful stage act, and soon attracted legions of fans. However, recording was less successful. Their first four-song release, on the tiny Uzi label, hardly sold. But it attracted the attention of famed record company boss David Geffen, who signed the band.

The first "proper" album was "Appetite For Destruction." An apt title, since the band seemed bent on causing huge problems for themselves through drugs, alcohol, sexist and racist comments, swearing and generally offensive behavior, which brought enormous and justified criticism. The first album took a year to reach No. 1 in the USA, although it has since sold more than 20 million copies. The next release was the live "G N' R Lies...," which captured the band's electrifying stage performance. In 1990 further alcohol problems forced Adler to leave. He was replaced by Matt Sorum, with Izzy Stradlin still on rhythm guitar.

"Appetite
For Destruction"
July '87
"G N' R Lies ..."
December '88

"Use Your Illusion I" and
"Use Your Illusion II"
September '91
"The Spaghetti Incident?"
November '93

W. Axl Rose cultivated his "bad boy" image.

NUMBERS ONE AND TWO

However, there were positive signs. Slash's reputation as a highly skilled guitarist gained recording invitations from Michael Jackson and other respected performers. In 1991 "Use Your Illusion I" reached No. 2 – beaten to the top spot by its co-release "Use Your Illusion II." G N' R have gradually matured into one of HM's greatest acts.

CUSTOM-MADE

Many heavy metal musicians have their instruments changed and modified to their own specifications, both in looks and sound. This is known as customizing. Slash of Guns N' Roses prefers a fairly basic Les Paul model (left), named after guitarist and recording innovator Les Paul, who designed the instrument in the 1950s for the Gibson company. Customizing can be as simple as changing the pick-ups on the guitar body to give a different type of sound. Gibson "Humbucker" pick-ups are renowned for their thick, fat sound, while Fender pick-ups produce sharper, slightly thinner tones. Or customizing may involve a guitar created entirely from specially designed parts, with a body in the shape of a moon, arrow or almost any other object. Some guitars become almost as famous as their players. Heavy rock band ZZ Top are renowned for their fur-covered "axes."

The "Super Yob" guitar built for Dave Hill of UK band Slade.

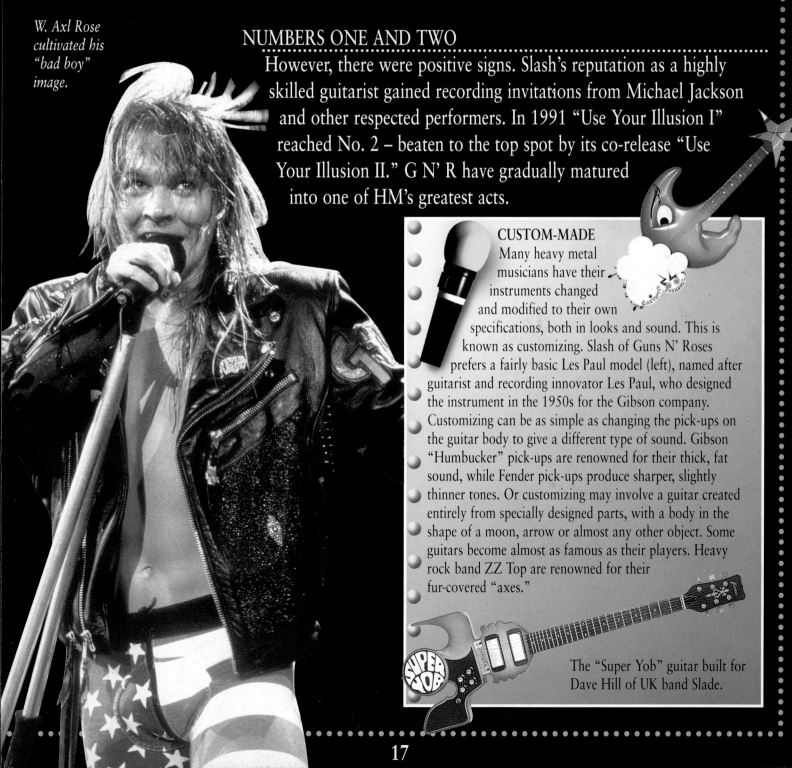

IRON MAIDEN

An "iron maiden" was a body-shaped cage used in medieval times, to restrain and torture victims. Iron Maiden the band played its first gig much later, in 1976. Bassist Steve Harris recruited Paul Di'Anno on vocals, Dave Murray on guitar, and drummer Doug Samson.

CONTINUING CHANGES

Over the years, Iron Maiden has changed line-up regularly. The first album in 1980 saw Dennis Stratton on guitar and Clive Burr on drums. It reached No. 4 in the UK. Maiden worked hard to promote it, and three of its tracks made Top 40 singles. But Harris was still not convinced. For the next album, "Killers," out went Stratton and in came Adrian Smith. British fans flocked to the band's gigs, but the USA took little notice.

NUMBER ONE, TIMES THREE

In 1980 Di'Anno left to form Lone Wolf. Sheffield-born Bruce Dickinson took over vocals, and the band had a Top 10 single "Run To The Hills" and their first of three chart-topping albums, "The Number Of The Beast." At last, the USA also took notice. In 1983 drummer Nicko McBain replaced Burr. Maiden toured extensively and between 1983 and '90, six of their albums made the UK Top 10. After a break in 1988, guitarist Janick Gers replaced Adrian Smith. In 1993, Bruce Dickinson went solo. Yet more changes have not dented Iron Maiden's momentum, and the band continues to hit the charts.

"Iron Maiden" April '80
"The Number Of The Beast" March '82
"Piece Of Mind" May '83
"Powerslave" September '84
"Somewhere In Time" September '86
"Seventh Son Of A Seventh Son" April '88
"Fear Of The Dark" May '92
"A Real Live One" March '93

Steve Harris (left) is Maiden's founder member.

KISS

Kiss were outrageous and glamorous. The name refers to the act between romantic lovers. But written in capital letters, KISS, it stood for the band's approach to its music, as in: "Keep It Simple, Stupid."

"Destroyer" May '76
"Dynasty" June '79
"Creatures Of The Night" October '82
"Lick It Up" September '83

"Animalise" September '84
"Asylum" September '85
"Crazy Nights" October '87
"Revenge" May '92
"Alive III" May '93

WALKING TALL

In the early 1970s, "glam rock" swept the modern music scene. Performers wore vivid make-up, glittering costumes and stack- or platform-soled boots. The trend spread to heavy metal, and one US band in particular took it to heart. They were Kiss, founded by bassist Gene Simmons (whose real name of Chaim Klein might seem more suited to the stage) and drummer Peter Criss.

KISS'S CRAZY NIGHTS

Kiss hit the charts with "Destroyer" in 1976. Simmons took the stack-soled boots fashion to new heights – about 23 inches. After moderate successes, the 1983 album "Lick It Up" achieved Top 10 status in the USA and UK. Kiss took their high-powered brand of glam-metal around the world on extensive tours.

In 1987 the album "Crazy Nights" was another huge hit, while the single from it, "Crazy Crazy Nights," has become a heavy rock classic.

19

LED ZEPPELIN

In the list of all-time greats in heavy music, Led Zeppelin would be near – or at – the top. They were born out of UK band the Yardbirds, whose line-ups had featured guitarists Eric Clapton and Jeff Beck.

Page (left) and Plant (right) still perform in the '90s.

In 1968 bass player John Paul Jones joined the band and became friends with its guitarist of the time, Jimmy Page. The two decided to form a new group.

SECOND-CHOICE SINGER

Page and Jones' first choice for singer was Terry Reid. He was tied up by contracts, but he recommended the virtually unknown Robert Plant. He, in turn, suggested immensely powerful drummer John "Bonzo" Bonham. The band name was provided by the Who's drummer, Keith Moon, who joked that they would "go down like a lead (leaden) zeppelin," referring to the ill-fated German airships.

SPEEDY SUCCESS

Lead became Led, and the quartet signed with Peter Grant, a manager with a fearsome reputation. As musicians, the band were already experienced.

"Led Zeppelin"
March '69
"Led Zeppelin II"
October '69
"Led Zeppelin III" October '70
"Led Zeppelin IV" November '71
"Houses Of The Holy" April '73

"Physical Graffiti" March '75
"Presence" April '76
"The Song Remains The Same" (live) October '76
"Remasters" (compilation)
October '90
"Boxed Set II" (compilation)
October '93

The first album with a Zeppelin airship.

Jimmy Page was a veteran of dozens of recordings, including Van Morrison's, as an anonymous "session guitarist." Jones had played with ex-Shadow Tony Meehan, and also with Plant in the Birmingham-based Band Of Joy. But the sheer speed of Led Zep's success surprised everyone. The first album in March 1969, released on the huge Atlantic label, shot into the Top 10 in Europe and the USA. It featured Page's stunning, blues-influenced playing, Plant's tortured vocals, Jones' solid bass and organ work and Bonham's massive drumming. Just eight months later, "Led Zeppelin II" topped charts around the world. It re-defined heavy rock music and is often quoted as the first true, riff-laden, heavy metal album. Zeppelin toured continually in their customized Boeing jetliner, performing spell-binding shows all over the world. Their anthem, the blues-rooted "Whole Lotta Love," was re-recorded by CCS and became the signature tune of the UK's long running TV show, "Top Of The Pops."

The second album has the band members "pasted" into the photograph.

STAIRWAY TO GREATNESS

By 1971 Led Zeppelin were demonstrating a more subtle, delicate approach. The album often referred to as Led Zep 4 or Symbols, but with the official title of four squiggle-like runes (ancient symbols), includes one of rock's greatest works. "Stairway to Heaven" begins with acoustic guitar and recorder. Zeppelin's second to sixth albums went straight to No. 1 in the UK and USA, a feat equaled by few others. 1976's "The Song Remains The Same" concert at New York's Madison Square Gardens captured the band on film. However, on Christmas Day 1980, John Bonham died after a drinking session. Zeppelin immediately disbanded, although Page and Plant have revisited their music in the 1990s.

MASTERS OF THE RIFF

Led Zeppelin, like many heavy metal and heavy rock bands, based their songwriting around riffs. A riff is a fairly short sequence of notes which is repeated throughout the song. The openings of Zep's "Whole Lotta Love" and Metallica's "Enter Sandman" are classic examples. The riff is usually played by the guitarist, and perhaps keyboardist, and often by the bassist too, for that "heavy" sound. It may be extended and developed in middle sections of the song, then re-stated in the closing sections. In a band with two on-stage guitarists, one may play the basic riff, while the other chooses notes in harmony and improvizes around it.

Page with twin-necked guitar (6 and 12 strings).

METALLICA

In 1981, Danish-born drummer Lars Ulrich and local guitarist-vocalist James Hetfield placed almost identical adverts in a Los Angeles music paper. Each wanted a "soul mate," a like-minded partner to develop a new metal band which would have the heaviest sound of all time. The two got together, clicked at once, and even agreed on the name for their new group.

A SHARED VISION

Hetfield and Ulrich began the search for band members to share their ideas. Ron McGovney joined on bass, but first guitarist Lloga Grand was quickly replaced by David Mustaine. By 1982 Mustaine also left, to develop his own career with thrash-metal band Megadeth. The next year, Cliff Burton came in as bassist. With Kirk Hammett on lead guitar, Ulrich and Hetfield were at last beginning to achieve the sound they wanted.

"Ride The Lightning"
July '84
"Master Of Puppets"
March '86
"And Justice For All"
September '88
"The Good, The Bad And The Live" May '90

"Metallica" (black album)
August '91
"Live Sh*t — Binge And Purge"
December '93
"Reload"
November '97

SUCCESS AND DISASTER

Metallica moved to the US East Coast and John Zazula's Mega Force label. The first albums, in 1984 and '86, caused few waves. But the band persevered, honing their extravagant and incredibly loud stage show.

Their songs were immensely powerful, dark and brooding, and drew musical comparisons with Black Sabbath. In 1986 "Master Of Puppets" broke into the Top 50. It seemed that five years of hard work were paying off at last. But in September '86, on tour in Sweden, the band bus crashed and bassist Cliff Burton died. Hetfield and Ulrich were tempted to finish, there and then. But they came around to the opinion that Burton would have wanted them to continue.

Cartoon heroes Beavis and Butthead are devoted Metallica fans.

Lead guitarist Hammett (above) and main singer Hetfield (left).

THE BLACK ALBUM

Metallica recruited Jason Newsted on bass. He did not try to copy his predecessor Burton, but brought his own voice, songwriting ideas and style of playing. In 1988, "And Justice For All" broke into the Top 10 album charts in the USA and UK. In 1991 the band struck gold, or rather, black. The black cover of the album "Metallica," with the snake logo in dark silver, means that this recording is known simply as the "black album" (a great honor, derived from the Beatles' "white album"). It made No. 1 in the USA, UK and most of Europe.

BENDING THE RULES

Metallica went on to bend and even break a few HM rules. They featured delicate harmonies and quiet passages. Their lyrics showed an open-minded, caring approach. They wrote protest songs against political and social injustice, while many other heavy bands refused to condemn such problems. In 1991, Metallica's storming performance at Donington's Monsters of Rock festival cemented their reputation as one of heavy metal's most thrilling, innovative, and LOUD bands.

IN THE STUDIO

Heavy metal is sometimes seen as a simple wham-crash-thud type of music. But for most HM bands, nothing could be further from the truth. Metallica's founders, Ulrich and Hetfield, could hear the distinctive sound they wanted in their heads. But it took several changes of band membership to come close. A final piece of the jigsaw was record producer Bob Rock. His sympathetic ear and wide experience helped to knit together the deep guitar and bass riffs and pounding drums, into one of HM's weightiest sounds.

The recording studio, where a band's "sonic signature" is developed.

MOTORHEAD

Colorful characters abound in heavy metal. After all, the music itself is larger than life, with its sheer power and intensity, and sometimes aggressive style. HM is rarely used as background music for a quiet dinner party! And characters are rarely more colorful than Motorhead's founder, bassist and singer, Lemmy.

A SHAKY BEGINNING

Ian Kilmister was born on Christmas Eve 1945, in Stoke-on-Trent, England – the son of a vicar. His nickname, Lemmy, came from his frequent pleas for money loans: "Lemme (lend me) a fiver!" Once a roadie for Jimi Hendrix, Lemmy was bass player in hippie-rock band Hawkwind from 1971. In 1975 he was fired after drug charges and keen for revenge, he formed his own band to play heavier, faster rock. The band name is slang for a person who takes amphetamine drugs ("speed").

FAST AND ANIMAL

After a false start with Larry Wallis and Lucas Fox, Lemmy's casual friend Phil "Animal" Taylor – who had limited experience but the right image – became his drummer. The power trio format was completed by experienced guitarist "Fast" Eddie Clarke. Motorhead would certainly not achieve overnight success. And they have never made a dent in the US album or singles charts.

"Motorhead" August '77
"Overkill" March '79
"Bomber" October '79
"Ace Of Spades" October '80
"No Sleep Til Hammersmith" June '81
"Ironfist" April '82

"Another Perfect Day" May '83
"No Remorse" (compilation) September '84
"Orgasmatron" July '86
"1916" January '91

But their frantic, energetic and sometimes deafening performances steadily built up large, enthusiastic audiences. In August 1977 their first album scraped into the UK Top 50. Three singles sold modestly and Motorhead's reputation slowly grew. In 1979 they made the UK Top 30 with the aptly named "Overkill."

FINALLY NUMBER ONE

In October the same year, the third album "Bomber" reached No. 12. Each release fared better until the band's second live album, "No Sleep Til Hammersmith," made No. 1. The 1980 single "Ace of Spades," from the same-name album, has become a metal classic. In 1982 Clarke left to form Fastway. Ex-Thin Lizzy guitarist Brian Robertson stepped in. The success of "Hammersmith" was never recaptured.

THE "TAP" ON TOUR
Heavy metal often seems to make fun of itself. Performers totter about on huge-heeled shoes, with theatrical stage make-up and extravagantly customized guitars. The fairground feel and tacky showmanship contribute to the sheer fun of it all. However in 1984 an achingly amusing film, "This Is Spinal Tap," provided the ultimate spoof on heavy rock. It is a fictional account of a distinctly fading band, Spinal Tap, and it sends up all aspects of the rock world. Ridiculously inflated egos, stupidly grandiose ideas, crooked managers, awful songwriting and dreadful record deals conspire to bring disaster at every turn. Like all good satire, the fiction is only slightly removed from the reality. Spinal Tap even turned themselves into a real band and toured to promote their spoof (but excellent) album "Break The Wind."

Actors turned heavy rockers of Spinal Tap.

In 1983 Robertson left. Guitarist Michael Burston, nicknamed "Wurzel" because of his resemblance to the children's fictional favorite, scarecrow-tramp Wurzel Gummidge, joined Phil Cambell and Lemmy. Taylor moved on, and drummer Pete Gill moved in. Lemmy thought another live album might provide a boost, but 1988's "No Sleep At All" only managed to scrape into the Top 100. Original drummer Taylor returned and, through the 1990s, Motorhead have continued their full-tilt approach – still one of British HM's best-loved bands.

THIN LIZZY

Thin Lizzy began in Dublin in 1969 – the brainchild of lanky, exotic-looking bass player and singer, Phil Lynott. Guitar player Eric Bell and drummer Brian Downey completed the trio. Phil had previously played in another Irish outfit, Skidrow. They were led by a 16-year old guitar star who would later achieve international fame, and be part of Thin Lizzy for a time. His name was Gary Moore.

MELODY TO METAL

Thin Lizzy started as a distinctly non-heavy band, playing a melodic mix of songs which reflected Lynott's Irish-Brazilian parentage. By 1972, the trio had two interesting but unsuccessful Decca albums behind them. Then came their tuneful but strong single "Whiskey In The Jar." It echoed their increasingly forceful direction, due in no small part to Lynott's powerful stage presence. It entered the UK Top 10 in January 1973, peaked at No. 6, and is still heard regularly. Lizzy moved further into heavy metal land, but the third album did not match the single's success. 1974 saw a succession of changes. Bell left and in came Phil Lynott's old Skidrow chum, Gary Moore. Not for long.

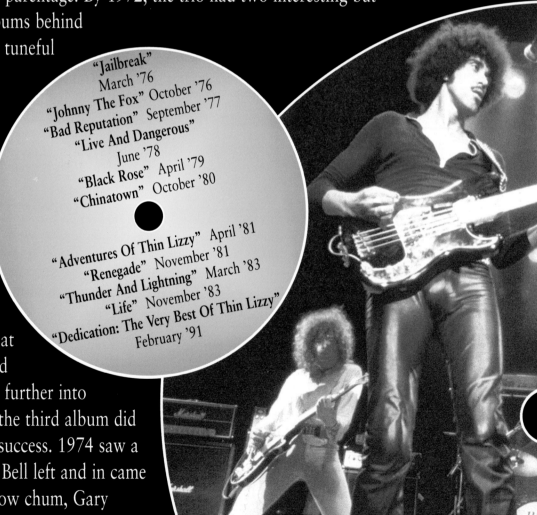

"Jailbreak"
March '76
"Johnny The Fox" October '76
"Bad Reputation" September '77
"Live And Dangerous"
June '78
"Black Rose" April '79
"Chinatown" October '80

"Adventures Of Thin Lizzy" April '81
"Renegade" November '81
"Thunder And Lightning" March '83
"Life" November '83
"Dedication: The Very Best Of Thin Lizzy"
February '91

The band regained its balance when Lynott took on Scott Gorham and Brian Robertson as twin lead guitarists. A lengthy tour of the UK enhanced Thin Lizzy's reputation as one of the more imaginative heavy bands. 1975's album "Fighting" was a minor hit, but the next one was massive. "Jailbreak" reached No. 10 in the UK and stayed in the album chart for a year. In May 1976 the single "The Boys Are Back In Town" went four places better – and also made the Top 20 in the USA.

LIVE AND DANGEROUS

In 1977, Brian Robertson was forced to take time out with a hand injury. Back came Gary Moore. The album "Bad Reputation" got to No. 4, and the following "Live and Dangerous" (1978), one of heavy rock's classic live performances, reached No. 2. However, bewildering personnel changes continued. Robertson left again; Moore returned again. In September 1979

Phil "Johnny the Fox" Lynott's heavy rock songs had romantic, folksy influences.

he was replaced by guitarist Midge Ure from Ultravox. In turn, he was replaced by Snowy White. Out came the excellent album "Chinatown," and the single of the same name gave Thin Lizzy their first No. 1. "Adventures Of Thin Lizzy," a compilation album, was yet another hit, but membership changes followed.

AN EARLY LOSS

"Thunder And Lighting" was released in 1983 and reached No. 4. However, in 1984 Phil Lynott decided that his band had run its course. He dissolved Thin Lizzy. Tragically, just two years later, he was dead. A charming and enigmatic man, and an intelligent song-crafter, Lynott sadly succumbed to drugs and alcohol addiction. He was just 35 years old.

DRUMS GALORE

Vocalists and guitarists often dominate the stage shows of heavy metal bands. Drummers are hidden behind their huge kits, unable to pose or rush about. Yet loud, solid drumming is the backbone of heavy rock. Rick Allen of Def Leppard is a fine example, but with a difference. He lost one arm in an accident. However, his specially customized kit enables him to carry on playing. Def Leppard have enjoyed more success in the USA than in their native UK.

Def Leppard are from Sheffield, England.

VAN HALEN

The riverside town of Nijmegen in Holland is the birthplace of two of the best-known heavy metal performers, Eddie (guitar) and Alex (drums) Van Halen. The brothers emigrated to the USA in the 1960s.

BORN TO ROCK

The Van Halen boys loved rock music, and teamed up with Chicago-born bass player Michael Antony and singer David Lee Roth, as Mammoth. Right from the start, they put everything into their loud, powerful, uncompromising metal music, performing in any Los Angeles venue, no matter how small. In the audience one night was Gene Simmons of Kiss (see page 19). He was impressed, especially with David Lee Roth's singing, and decided to help. But the name Mammoth was already taken by another band. After dismissing Rat Salade, the band decided that they would be known simply as Van Halen. Simmons introduced them to producer Ted Templeman, who quickly signed them to Warner Brothers. Van Halen's first album, released in early 1978, entered the Top 40 on both sides of the Atlantic. Over the following year it sold more than two million copies around the world.

THE HEAVY BASS

One of the defining sounds of heavy metal music is the low notes of the bass guitar, often thudding in time to the bass drum. The bassist can repeat the basic notes of the key, for a solid, unfussy foundation to the song, or follow the notes of the other guitarists to emphasize the riffs. Playing bass seems an easy option, compared to a frontman vocalist or guitarist. But the bassist must stay in perfect synchronization with the drummer, or the bedrock of the HM sound loses its kick and punch.

Rick Savage plays bass in Def Leppard.

The success of Van Halen was due partly to David Lee Roth's stunning singing and outrageous stage presence. He captivated audiences with his wild-man antics and over-the-top performances. More importantly, his vocals also sounded great in the more demanding environment of the recording studio, where small variations in tone and key become far more obvious. In 1978, Eddie Van Halen was named as Best New Guitarist by the influential American magazine, "Guitar Player." But the band's early singles did less well. They had to wait until the release of their second album, in April 1979, before their fifth single made the Top 20 in the USA.

"Van Halen"
April '78
"Van Halen II" April '79
"Women And Children First" March '80
"Fair Warning" May '81
"Diver Down" May '82
"1984" January '84

"5150" March '86
"OU812" June '88
"Live: Right Here, Right Now"
February '93
"Balance" January '95
"Van Halen III" March '98

David Lee Roth had a hit solo album in 1991 with "A Little Ain't Enough."

JUMPING INTO THE CHARTS

In 1979 the group's spectacular rise to fame moved into top gear. "Van Halen II" sold better than their first album. The momentum continued for six years, with four more Top 50 albums. Only five of their 13 singles cracked the Top 20. But one was "Jump" – their first No. 1. The album that carried it, "1984," stayed in the US Billboard charts for a year. However, in 1985 the band reverted to a trio when dynamic David Lee Roth left to try his luck solo. Next year a new singer appeared – Sammy Hagar from HM band Montrose. The first single featuring Hagar went to No. 3 in the USA. The album "5150" (which is the US police code for prisoners considered insane) became their first of four US No. 1s, although it only reached No. 16 in the UK. Van Halen have continued to enjoy worldwide success, filling huge stadiums with their extravagant, exciting stage shows. Eddie Van Halen also made an impressive guest appearance on one of the biggest-selling albums of all time, Michael Jackson's 1982 "Thriller."

GAZETTEER

Since the 1960s, heavy metal music has diversified into many different forms. A book like this cannot detail the hundreds of top-class "heavy" performers through the years. Selected bands shown here demonstrate the many styles of heavy rock music.

The Gibbons brothers of ZZ Top.

HEAVY BOOGIE

The term "heavy rock" includes a wide variety of loud, energetic music styles, featuring mainly guitar, bass guitar and drums, and perhaps keyboards. Texan band ZZ Top play "heavy metal boogie," based around the 12-bar blues format widely used in boogie and rock 'n' roll. Their 1983 album "Eliminator," with their trademark red custom car, sold millions. In the 1970s, British group Nazareth also played a basic rock beat with plentiful slide guitar. They had a Top 10 album, "Loud 'n' Proud," in 1973.

HEAVY ROCK

More varied and theatrical is the music of Meatloaf. Working with acclaimed record producer and

songwriter Jim Steinman, his recordings have long songs with many different sections, changing in pace and rhythm and featuring piano passages, trumpets and even violins. His massive seller "Bat Out Of Hell," released in 1978, has spent a total of nine years in the Top 100 album chart. The follow-up "Bat Out Of Hell II – Back Into Hell" reached No. 1 in 1993.

Meatloaf's original name was Marvin Lee Aday.

Another hugely successful band are Rush, from Canada. They had six Top 10 albums in the 1980s.

Rush hit the big time with "Permanent Waves" in 1980.

Nazareth's 1973 single "Broken Down Angel" made the UK Top 10.

Their style is loud and heavy, yet melodic. The tunes are catchy and some have a quieter, more romantic feel. This type of music, with a wider appeal, is termed AOR, adult-orientated rock. One of AOR's most popular performers is former recording studio janitor, Jon Bon Jovi. He is leader-singer-songwriter-guitarist in the band that bears his name. Since "New Jersey" in 1988, each Bon Jovi album has reached No. 1. Jon has also written movie soundtracks such as "Young Guns II."

John Francis Bongiovi Junior – alias Jon Bon Jovi.

GRUNGE

A new type of heavy music appeared in about 1990. Known as grunge, it is weighty but generally fairly slow, with a scowling, grinding feel, very distorted guitar sounds, growled vocals and angry lyrical content. Widely successful grunge bands include Seattle-based Nirvana, whose 1991 album "Nevermind" helped to define the sound, and Smashing Pumpkins. Sadly Nirvana's vocalist-guitarist Kurt Cobain shot himself in 1994 in a fit of deep depression.

OTHER "METALS"

There are many other kinds of metal-based heavy music. Thrash metal is played almost excessively fast. Death metal, whose performers include Brazilian band Sepultura, is obsessed with dying, skulls, skeletons, coffins and graveyards. No doubt other exciting, energetic "metals" will appear in future years.

Smashing Pumpkins

Sepultura write about social issues in their homeland.

INDEX

PHOTOGRAPHIC CREDITS Abbreviations: *t-top, m-middle, b-bottom, r-right, l-left, c-center*
Front cover c & br, 6bl, 7l, 8tl, 14m, 18-19, 21b, 22 & 29b - E. Reberts/Redferns. Cover bl, 7r, 9m, 11 both, 14t, 19 both, 24tl, 26t, 26-27, 27t, 28t, 29t, 30b & 31t - F. Costello/Redferns. Cover bm, 3, 6m, 8bl, 8-9, 12t & br, 16b, 18b, 25l, 27b, 28br, 30t, 31mr & b - M. Hutson/Redferns. 4-5 & 12bl - R. Aaron/Redferns. 5tl - E. Echenberg/Redferns. 6tl & 31ml P. Ford/Redferns. 10t - Gems/Redferns. 10m - S. Ritter/Redferns. 10b, 14-15 & 15t - A. Putler/Redferns. 13t - C. Stewart/Redferns. 13m - K. Morris/Redferns. 13b - Michael Ochs Archive/Redferns. 15b, 21tl & tr & 30m - Redferns. 20t - T. Hanley/Redferns. 20b - I. Dickson. 23t - Frank Spooner Pictures. 22-23 - G. DeSota/Redferns. 23m - M. Linssen/Redferns. 23b - S. Gibbons/Redferns. 24m - P. Cronin. 25r - Embassy Films (courtesy Kobal Collection).